Hello Ladies!

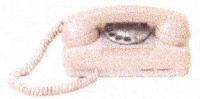 

I0528607

I see you. I know you. Because I am you.

An independent modern woman focusing on being everything to everyone, balancing work, love, life & still hoping to find time to strengthen and explore a personal relationship with the man upstairs.

It can be difficult, frustrating, and downright overwhelming - not to mention, sometimes reading the good book, doesn't make as much sense as we'd like it to.

Which is why I've created *Everyday Devotions & Journal*, 90 bitesize **daily devotions** complete with the word of God, restyled in a way that makes sense and resonates with the modern woman, a quick **interpretation** to help connect the timeless wisdom of our Heavenly Father with the modern age, a **prayer** written especially for us ladies to restart a conversation with God our father, and **prompts** meant to help you reflect on how the word of God relates to your own daily life.

Remember, you're exactly who and where you need to be. Your life, is no accident. No matter how messy it may seem. God, the Father, has a plan for you, for each of us.

XOXO
Lisa

Everyday Devotions & Journal

90 daily devotions & journal prompts for modern women seeking to strengthen & explore their personal relationship with God

Lisa Marie Heath

Author of *Life of Lisa: Overcoming Adversity With Love and Laughter*

Everyday Devotions & Journal

is a work of my own creation.

The information in this book was correct at the time of publication, and the Author does not assume any liability for loss or damage caused by errors or omissions, again, this is my perspective, opinion, and experience, so it has been written as such.

Copyright © 2024 by Lisa Marie Heath

All rights reserved.

No part of this book may be reproduced or transmitted in any form or by any means, electronic or mechanical, including photocopying, recording, or by any information and retrieval systems, without the written permission of the Publisher, except where permitted by law.

ISBN - 978-1-961185-42-5

Cover, Book Design, and Layout by megs thompson
megswrites llc - www.megswrites.com

www.inomniaparatuspublishing.com

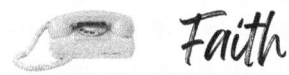
Faith

God looked across the table at Satan and setting down his grande quad-shot americano he asked, "Well, have you ever thought about my boy Job? He's a real mans-man, takes care of his family, always gets to work on time, is a straight shooter, a huge animal lover, and has a healthy balance of love & fear for me."

Job 2:3 LOLV

Interpretation:

Have you ever wondered why God singled out Job? Like, really? Job did nothing wrong. But as God sat there chatting with Satan, he pointed out his devoted follower, Job, why? Because of his faith. Not Job's faith in God, but God's faith in Job. He knew, through faith, that he could and would do, what was right. What was needed. God believes in us too. Each and every one of us, no matter who we are, what we do in life, or how long we've known him. God wasn't putting Job in a position to fail, he was setting him up to succeed in the highest form of glory Now it may have sucked, don't get me wrong, but overall, God's faith in us will always be more powerful than anything Satan can send our way.

Prayer:

Dear Heavenly Father, I've seen what you can do through other people who have faith in you. Thank you for always having faith in me and trusting that I'll do the right thing. In your name. Amen.

Reflection: How does it make you feel, to read that God singled Job out during his coffee-date with Satan? Do you ever find yourself questioning the load you've been given by God?

Peace

Hey! God here. Rest easy and don't fill your mind with worries about the world, the news, politics, or what celebrities are starring on the next season of Dancing With The Stars. I'm here with you, beside you, holding your hand, and comforting your every fear. *Isaiah 41:10-13 LOLV*

Interpretation:

Have you ever noticed how our mind is filled with the worldly things around us? How much time do you spend decompressing? God realizes that and knows that we need his hand, his arm, and his chest, to relax into. To rest. To calm and comfort us. When was the last time you let yourself lay down and allowed God to take care of you? Enjoying the peace that settles into our soul the way only God can provide.

Prayer:

God, thank you for being the man that you are. For being beside me, holding my hand and making sure that I'm okay. I'm perfectly made the way you want me to be. The outside world is simply an influence, a temptation, to take me off pace of where I am, with you. Please allow these words to show how I stand here, today, conquering my world, with you. Amen.

Reflection:

What are your fears? Have you handed those over to God? Why not? Having fears is not being in peace. Release your fears onto the pages below and ask the Lord to receive them, filling you with love and peace.

 *Courage*

Ladies, be bold and courageous, fear not, for the Lord your God goes with you. He'll never let you down or abandon you.

Deuteronomy 31:6 LOLV

Interpretation:

There isn't much to explain here ladies. God created us to be bold, to be courageous, to live the life he's intentionally set out for us. Sure, it can seem scary to stand up and stand out at times, but no matter what, we're never alone. We never really need to be afraid. God is with us. Always.

Prayer:

Dear Lord, bless today as I step out in courage, as bold as can be! With your strength I will not fear the unknown of today's events. In your name. Amen.

Reflection:

What fears are holding you back being the woman God sees you as? If God is with us everywhere we go (which he is), why not speak those fears out loud, or jot them down for him to read over your shoulder? Then, when you have the time to address them with God, you may find that He already has a plan in place for you. Stay bold and courageous.

 *Dance*

My heart's doing the happy dance, and my tongue's throwing a party! My whole body is chilling in ultimate peace and security. Life is good.

Psalm 16:9 LOLV

Interpretation:
God celebrates every win. That includes just waking up and getting out of bed sometimes. As you go through the day, what little wins can you do a happy dance to celebrate? That chill excited feeling you have... the tingle... it's God's love. He'll never, never, never, ever forsake you.

Prayer:
Lord, every time I hear a song today, I'm going to do a little dance with and for you. Life is good when we're doing it together. Thank you for always being my partner, on and off the dance floor. Amen.

Reflection:
What's your initial reaction when something good happens? Is it happy, overwhelming, or is it the opposite? What if no matter what happened in life, you did a little dance. Whether you do or you don't, you'll have to deal with things, so why not get into that good feeling flow and experience the love God has in store for you with an impromptu dance party!

 *Alone*

Jesus swoops in to rescue us, adopting us as a part of his crew. We're officially God's kids' meaning that we'll never really be alone.

Galatians 4:5-6 LOLV

Interpretation:
You remember that song from the 90s? The one that says, "You are not alone...I am here with you?" Well, that could basically be God's theme song for us. Even when we feel most lonely, when we feel like no one is listening or cares what's going on in our crazy lives, God does. He's always listening, always waiting for us to share our thoughts with him. To tell him what's bugging us, or giving us headaches.

Prayer:
Dear Lord, Thank you for always being here to talk to, to bounce ideas off, and to share my crazy thoughts. With you in my life, I am never alone. In your name. Amen.

Reflection:

When do you feel most alone? What are you doing? Is it when you're feeling stressed, overwhelmed, or sad? Remember that God is always there, waiting for you to talk to him. He wants to keep us company, and hear about our lives.

 *Dreams*

Hey, queens, let's chat. Planning your future is cool, but remember, tomorrow's a mystery. So, dream big, but let God's plan take the lead.

James 4:13-14 LOLV

Interpretation:
I personally have a dream board that I look at every single day. This is how I plan and dream for the future. I may not know exactly how things are going to happen yet, but God does. What I tackle daily, are my little dreams, moving toward the bigger dream that God has planned for me. Always remember, dream big, but never lose sight of the simple thing, the days out with friends, the spontaneous adventures, the silver linings.

Prayer:
Lord, I am so happy that you're taking the lead and planning the most intimate details of my future. I love knowing that all I have to do is wake up and make today the best day possible. Thank you for giving me the ability to dream, and know that with you, nothing is impossible. Amen.

Reflection:

As James stated, "Let God take the lead." Where in your life are you not yet letting God take the lead? What things are you still trying to control yourself? What little things can you give control of, to God? It's scary, but think about your big crazy dreams, how are these little pieces contributing to that? Are they holding you back? If so, give them to God.

 Truth

Keep it real, peeps! Don't let any nasty words slip past those lips of yours. Only dish out what helps others, suiting their vibe. It's all about benefitting the folks tuned into your conversation.

Ephesians 4:29 LOLV

Interpretation:
We've all been in those situations. Where someone cuts you off in traffic, grabs the last pair of shoes in your size, or generally acts like a fool. Those moments where we want to embrace our gritty side and curse them out, call them a name, or flip them the bird. We get those urges because we're human, but God also created us in his image, meaning we possess the ability to turn the other cheek. We get to choose how we're going to react, or not. What we're going to say, or not. And whether we mutter curses, or a quick prayer, asking that God shine a light in their life, the way he's shining in ours.

Prayer:
Dear Lord, Thank you for having patience with me. Even on those days where I'm acting out, or being petty, thank you for never giving up on me, and for always staying in my corner, reminding me that it's never too late to turn things around. In your name. Amen.

Reflection:

When was the last time you flipped out and said something you regretted? We've all done it, but it's what we do next that really matters. Are you quick to apologize and talk through the situation? How might you be able to better pause and choose the words that you use in times of passion?

 *Friends*

Listen up, queens! Everything, and I mean everything, was created through and for our ultimate bff, Jesus. He's the real deal - no if's, and's, or but's.

Colossians 1:16 LQLV

Interpretation:
Ladies, God is the truest friend you could ever desire. Never judging us, while always holding our hand. Friends will come and go throughout our lives but the one who will never leave is the big man upstairs. Talk to him, about everything. All he wants is for us to be his friends and let him into our daily lives. No matter what you say, no matter the topic of conversation, he's listening. I promise.

Prayer:
Jesus, I love that you think so much of me, and ensure that I never walk through life without a friend. I'm forever grateful. In your name. Amen.

Reflection:

Have you ever felt like your friends don't understand what you're saying? What have you done in the past when you've been faced with those feelings? Jesus really is the best friend a girl can have. How do you communicate with him, to keep that relationship strong?

Trust

Ladies, embrace humility under God's mighty hand, and in due time, he'll lift you up. Hand over all of your cares, worries, and fears to him. He has always, and will always, have your best interest in mind.

1 Peter 5:6 LOLV

Interpretation:

As women we often find ourselves carrying the burdens of our own lives as well as those of our families, friends, and coworkers. It's important that we always remember, while we may be strong and independent women, we're never doing this thing called life alone. God is always there to support us, lift us up, and take all of our worries and cares away. It's a matter of us trusting in him.

Prayer:

Jesus, I know that I need to trust in you more. I'm working on that, along with trusting myself. Give me grace to overcome the fears I have around trusting. In your name. Amen.

Reflection:

Are you someone who enjoys carrying a heavy load? Whether at home, at work, with your friends, or maybe all of the above. Why is it you do this? Is it because you feel alone, or do you have a hard time trusting others? God isn't just a regular friend - he's THE friend, the one we can trust with anything and everything.

 Thanks

Girl, keep your heart uncluttered from the love of money. Be happy with what you've got, 'cause He promised that he'll never bail on you or let you down.

Hebrews 13:5 LOLV

Interpretation:
We've all heard the phrase, "robbing Peter to pay Paul." For the longest time, I lived my life in pursuit of money, earning it, spending it, sharing it. That was until I realized that money isn't love. The desire for money, is a distraction from the love God, our father, offers us in abundant, limitless quantities. Be thankful for the Lord's promise of abundance, and trust in the never ending love he has for you. Money, will come and go, but the Lord will provide for your needs in the right time and way.

Prayer:
Dear Heavenly Father. Thank you for showing me a different view of money. I'm beyond happy knowing that you'll never let me down or leave me needing. I give you my heart and trust in this and all things. In your name. Amen.

Reflection:

What issues, concerns, worries, or frustrations have you experienced with money? Where has your relationship with money gone awry? Do you find yourself robbing Peter to pay Paul? Be real for a moment, where has this gotten you? Instead, think about money as grace. Where in your life can you focus on increasing the grace in your life?

 *Rest*

On the seventh day, God wrapped up his masterpiece and took a well-deserved break. He blessed the day, made it special, and chilled out after all of the amazing work he'd done.

Genesis 2:2-3 LOLV

Interpretation:

God was right, after working SO hard, to take a break, to rest. He set this example for us on the importance of resting. Too often in life we push ourselves to the brink of exhaustion, without allowing ourselves the grace of rest. When was the last time you took an hour, a day, a weekend, a week, to rest, to appreciate the life you have, the things you've accomplished? To be at our best, to truly honor God and all that he's created, we owe it to him, and ourselves, to rest.

Prayer:

Dear Heavenly Father. I may not be the best at resting, but I ask that you continue to remind me to rest, to take a break, from my life, my work, my friends, my family. Thank you for setting such an amazing example for me. In your name. Amen.

Reflection:
God was able to accomplish EVERYTHING in 6 days, taking a single full day to rest. What areas of your life, what obligations, are you placing above the importance of rest? Surely, you aren't creating a whole new world. How can you show yourself grace by taking a moment to rest today, this week? God prioritized rest, so should we.

Love

Girlfriends, it's not just about talking the talk; it's about walking the walk. God's heart is all about genuine love, not just lip service.

Matthew 15:8 LOLV

Interpretation:
I don't know how much more there is to dig into this one ladies. God wants us to be real, authentic, fully 100% who we are - not only in how we act, but in what we say. None of that lip service shenanigans or speaking out of both sides of our mouths. Nope. We get to live our lives wholly who we are, as proud children of God. Women, on a mission, to spread the love of God everywhere we go, to everyone we meet.

Prayer:
Dear Lord, Please help me to remain authentic and true in all areas of my life. Thank you for always guiding me and showering me with your love. In your name. Amen.

Reflection:

Do you ever find yourself changing how you act, or the things you say, when you're in the company of certain people? It can be easy to get wrapped up in the materialistic parts of our world, putting on a show to fit in. How can you better align your thoughts, words, and action to remain truthful and genuine at all times?

 *Gossip*

Babe, steer clear of the gossip queens. The one who spills secrets and flatters with smooth talk? She's not someone you want to mess with.

Proverbs 20:19 LOLV

Interpretation:
Nothing good ever comes from gossip. That includes speaking it, listening to it, and being in the presence of those who spread it. So, don't bother yourself with that kind of life ladies. Besides, if she's talking gossip about someone else while you're there, what's she saying about you when. you're not? God has always got our back and will never leave us alone, so when the gossip starts flowing, excuse yourself and find more aligned company.

Prayer:
Dear Heavenly Father, Thank you for creating me with the sense to know what's right and what's wrong, good and bad. Please continue to arm me with the confidence to leave negative and gossip-filled situations. In your name. Amen.

Reflection:

Are there people or a group of people that you spend time with who always seem to be spreading the latest gossip? Have you ever asked them to stop, or brought up that gossip is something with zero positive outcomes? No one likes being talked about, but it takes a strong woman to stand up and say so.

Future

Hey doll, your future is shining bright! No cutting off of your hope – it's here to stay.

Proverbs 23:18 LOLV

Interpretation:
No matter who you are, how old you are, where you live in the world, there will be days that are better than others. And, that means there will be days that, to be completely honest, are going to suck! But, your future is shining bright! God has a plan specifically for YOU, no one else. Keep your head held high, your chin up, and trust that when the time is right, he'll share all of his plans with you.

Prayer:
Dear Heavenly Father, as the sun comes up, I know that every day you are with me. Allow me to do my best for what is best for me & to seek out options that are in my best interest to serve my purpose here. In your name. Amen.

Reflection:
When you were little, what did you want to be when you grew up? What were your thoughts or dreams about the future? How have your ideas about the future changed as you've aged? What habits or hobbies do you have now that are helping your future self be the best version they can be?

 Speak

Girl, if you're speaking a language people don't understand, how will they catch your drift? You might as well be whispering into the wind.

1 Corinthians 14:9 LOLV

Interpretation:
Do you ever find yourself sitting at a restaurant or a park and hearing snippets of the conversations happening around you? I know for me personally, when this happens and the people chatting are from a younger generation, I'm often absolutely lost about what it is they're actually saying. That's how it is when we're trying to share God's message in a way that people don't understand. The answer, is to share how God's word, his love, his guidance, have touched your life. The truth about God and his unwavering support, that spans all possible language barriers.

Prayer:
Dear Heavenly Father, bless every interaction I have today with kindness to show others your love, through me. In your name. Amen.

Reflection:

How has your relationship with God shaped and changed your life? How can you live a life that shows this? When you're living a life that's been touched by God, it's obvious from miles away and often speaks louder than words.

 *Tears*

Sis, the tears that lead us away from wrong and into God's arms bring salvation. No regrets there. But the kind of tears tied to worldly sorrow? That's a spiritual dead end, so steer clear.

2 Corinthians 7:10 LOLV

Interpretation:
It's a part of our nature to feel sorrow, to cry, and scream. God created us to feel emotions, all of them, but he also designed a world where we're given the freedom to choose between following the path he has for us, or giving into temptation. I'll let you in on a little secret. The path of temptation is filled with far more tears and sorrow, than the path laid by God.

Prayer:
Lord, I have forsaken you, and for that I am sorry. I'm sorry that I've doubted you. I'm sorry that I haven't seen the path you've laid in front of me. I'm thankful that you've never given up on me. Because today, I shine brighter than ever before. In your name, Amen.

Reflection:

When in your life have you felt the most sorrow? Was it due to decisions you made that were following your earthly desires, or the path set out by God? What have you learned from those experiences? How are you a stronger woman today?

 **Plans**

Girl, before you even took your first breath, God had his eye on you. He knew you inside out, and He's got big plans for your beautiful soul.

Jeremiah 1:5 LOLV

Interpretation:
It's true, before you were born, before your parents had met, heck, before your grandparents were born, God knew of his plan for you. He knew what you would look like, how many hairs would be on top of your head, and when you would get your first tattoo. He knew it all, because he created you by design. So, live life, praise God, love one another, and wake up every morning ready to experience the amazing plans he has in store.

Prayer:
Dear Heavenly Father. I know you built me in your image and created me exactly how I am. Forgive me for the thoughts I have about myself. I do see the worthiness & beauty within myself that you do. Allow me to continue seeing myself as you see me. In your name, Amen.

Reflection:

It's crazy to think about someone knowing everything about you - more than you even know yourself, but it's true. God knows everything about us, the good and the not so stellar, and he loves us all the same. Do you have an idea of the plans God has set out for you?

 *Humble*

Squad, channel your inner Jesus. Keep a humble vibe, think of others before yourself, and show grace.

Philippians 2:5-8 LOLV

Interpretation:
Ladies, God has created each and every one of us with our own unique gifts and talents but that doesn't mean he wants us getting all braggy about them. Trust me, when we remain humble, sharing our gifts and special abilities with the world as God shares his light with us, that's what makes him happiest.

Prayer:
Dear Heavenly Father, Please help me to stay humble. I am forever grateful for the unique gifts and talents you've given me. I desire to use them to praise you and share your word and your message with the world. In your name. Amen.

Reflection:

What skills or talents are you most proud of? How do you utilize these attributes on a daily basis? Do you find yourself bragging about these special things you can do that others cannot or do you feel comfortable sharing your talents with others, without a need for recognition?

 Sparkle

Hey, amazing ladies, you're chosen by God, a royal squad, a holy clique, His own special crew. You're here to light up the world with your sparkle.

1 Peter 2:9 LOLV

Interpretation:

Have you ever been to a sporting event and found yourself watching the sometimes annoying, over-bubbly cheerleaders? I know I have. There just seems to be a little too much pep in their step. But, I've got something to tell you. That my friends, that's sparkle! Now, they may be using their sparkle to cheer on a team or player, but we get to use our sparkle to cheer on our favorite player, the real MVP. God. We're here to light up not only our own lives, the lives of our family, and friends, but to share our sparkle with strangers. So, get out there girlfriend. Sparkle like you mean it!

Prayer:

Lord, you created me to be a unique amazing woman. Thank you for seeing me, for hearing me, and for empowering me to live a life worthy of your grace. In your name. Amen.

Reflection:

While you may not like being in the spotlight you can still sparkle. No, you don't need to stand in front of a crowd or be on TV, you can sparkle right in the comfort of your home. How can you sparkle a little bit more today? Maybe it's in how you interact with your neighbors, your family, or the checker at the grocery store. It's amazing how much an extra smile can help boost the world around you. Go forth & sparkle.

 *Sacrifice*

Sisters, let's talk about the ultimate sacrifice. Jesus, the precious one, was handed over according to God's plan. It's a wild love story.

Acts 2:23 LOLV

Interpretation:

Can you even imagine making the kind of sacrifice God made in allowing his only son to die for the sins of the world? I know that I can't. He did this because of the intense love he has for us, his sinful children. And yet, no matter how many bad choices or wrong turns we make in life, never once does he regret the sacrifice he made.

Prayer:

Dear Heavenly Father, you've been through it all and here I sit, thanking you for everything you've gone through. For it is only through you that I'm able to be here today, and I am forever thankful. In your name. Amen.

Reflection:

When in your life have you made sacrifices? Have they been to protect others? Yourself? To achieve something you really wanted? How has it felt, to make such a sizable sacrifice? Have you ever had someone else make a sacrifice for your wellbeing or happiness? Aside from God of course.

 *Time*

Queens, life's a beautiful dance. There's a time for everything, a season for every purpose under the sun. Embrace the rhythm!

Ecclesiastes 3:1 LOLV

Interpretation:
Chill out ladies. Take a breath. Embrace the rhythm of this beautiful dance we call life. God has created time and seasons for us to fully embrace the rhythm of our lives. He wants us to have a blast, to enjoy life, to not worry, to not compare ourselves to anyone else, and instead, to move in our bodies. To be grateful and proud of where we are, who we are. Stand up, shake it out, do a little dance.

Prayer:
Praise the Lord, today is a new day. Thank you Jesus for waking me up with your shine and allowing your glory to show through me today. In your name. Amen.

Reflection:

Next time you're alone, feeling stressed or overwhelmed, move your body. When we stop moving, our lives stop, our rhythm pauses, and we lose the momentum of the magic we're creating. Have you ever thought about how time goes by super slowly or extremely fast, depending on what you're doing? What seasons in your life have gone slow or fast? How can you change what you're doing, how you're living to experience more of the rhythm & less of the song breaks?

 *Calm*

Jesus gives us a unique and powerful kind of peace – not like the temporary peace the world hands out. Let your hearts stay calm; fear and troubles have no place here.

John 14:27 LOLV

Interpretation:
I have a unique way of looking at this idea. I'm a person of nature, I love being out in the woods or by the water. Cities are always buzzing, and you never get a truly quiet moment to be fully calm and at peace. The best places that I've found have been walks with my dog while listening to an audiobook, educating me on the conditions I've been diagnosed with; breathing in the fresh air and knowing that I was alone, just me, my dog, God, and the voice in my ear. Whenever I start to feel like the world is giving me temporary peace, I always revert back to nature, and a brisk walk. With each breath in, I fill my lungs with calm, with peace.

Prayer:
Lord, as I go out into the world today, I want the type of peace and calm that you provide. I don't want the temporary peace of the world, I want to hold your hand, and stay calm in the storm. I want to remember that I have nothing to fear. Sometimes, staying calm can be hard, and I may need a little extra grace, but I'm doing my best. In your name. Amen.

Reflection:

What's a unique place where you've found peace and calm? Can you visualize it? How many details can you remember, what did it smell like, sound like, feel like? On days when you can't physically visit your place, being able to visit in your mind, from your bed, car, or couch, can provide a sense of calm to reconnect with the Lord.

 *Fearless*

Queens, listen up! Be bold and fearless, for the Lord, your God is right by your side wherever you go. No need for fear; God's got your back.

Joshua 1:9 LOLV

Interpretation:
Hey Friend. What are you afraid of? Spoiler, the answer should be nothing. Now, I'm not talking about reasonable fear, like jumping out of planes or standing in the middle of the road, but the big fear. We have no reason to fear life, to dress how we want, to dance how we want, to be ourselves. So what if you out-sparkle someone, or laugh a little too loud? The opinions of others that we so often fear, should never stop us from being who God created us to be. So, get out of your own head, put those shiny big girl pants on, and start living your bold, fabulous, fearless life.

Prayer:
Dear God. Allow me to choose the best option for me today. I know that looking out for myself is the first step & the second step is allowing you to work on my behalf. In your name. Amen.

Reflection:

Where in your life are you fearing the judgement of others when the only opinion that matters is the big man upstairs. Like Josh said, God wants this for us, he wants us to be the most unique, authentic, genuine, version of ourselves. Now think about this, who are you really here for? Like, on Earth. Who are you trying to impress, and where in your life can you be a little bit more fearless?

 Gifts

Ladies, open your ears when I say that God didn't give us fear; He gave us power, love, and a sound mind.

2 Timothy 1:7 LOLV

Interpretation:
God gives each of us countless different gifts, but one trait we all share that was not a gift from him, was fear. The devil seeks to take away everything pure and amazing in our lives, which includes our relationship with God. He's the reason we experience fear, challenging us to lose faith and not trust that God has a plan for us, that we can believe we'll be taken care of, and safe. Remember ladies, how powerful you are - and that your power, comes directly from God.

Prayer:
Dear Lord, please provide me with the clarity to recognize, embrace, and use the gifts you've given me. When and if I experience fear, please help me to see the best way through it, to bring me even closer to you. In your name. Amen.

Reflection:

We all have gifts, or as I like to call them, superpowers. I may be dating myself here, but it makes me feel like a Power Ranger. What unique gifts or superpowers do you have? What things come easy to you? What do you enjoy doing most? Keep these things in mind, because they aren't simply talents or skills you possess, they're genuine gifts from God. That's a big deal ladies!

Prayer

Beloved queens, pray with confidence. If your heart aligns with God's will, He hears you. So, speak your heart, knowing He's listening and responding.

1 John 5:14 LOLV

Interpretation:
Remember ladies, God is the best friend we could ever desire. He wants to hear from us, all the time. Pray to him, sharing your worries, frustrations, excitement, happiness, all of it - he wants to hear it all. By speaking your heart you're able to better connect with God on a deeper level, solidifying the sacred connection between you.

Prayer:
Dear Heavenly Father, I may not speak to you as often as I'd like but know that I'm forever grateful for your compassion, kindness, and love. In your name. Amend.

Reflection:

Do you talk to God daily? Sometimes we feel like in order to talk to God, we have to do it in a church, from our needs, or at a specific time of day. The truth is that God wants to hear from us at all times, in all places, about everything. So, next time you're in the car enjoying a warm spring day, or in your garden planting flowers, have a chat with God. He's always listening and wants to hear what's on your heart.

 *Besties*

Queens, here's the lesson: Use your resources to benefit others, make lasting friendships. When earthly possessions fade, these friends will welcome you to an eternal home.

Luke 16:9 LOLV

Interpretation:
We've all heard the saying, "A rising tide lifts all boats." Well, it's true. We're stronger when we work together, supporting and encouraging each other, than we are if we compete with each other. Keep this in mind not only in friendships, but business as well. By working together, sharing our knowledge and resources, we're able to succeed together.

Prayer:
Dear Lord, Thank you for providing me with friends and colleagues who want to work together for the great good of all involved. Please continue to help me see ways in which we can all succeed and thrive. In your name. Amen.

Reflection:

Do you find yourself choosing to work alone versus with a group or a team? What skills and resources do you possess that you might be able to share with a group to achieve something bigger together than you would on your own?

 *Faith*

When he heard the devastating news, Job flipped out. He started tearing at his clothes & shaved off his hair (Brittany-style). But then, Job pulled himself together & dropped to his knees to chat with God. "Hey God. It's me, Job. I get it, I was born naked & will die the same. You're the big-man upstairs, the guy in charge & the badass that gave me the life I have, my family, my home, my health, hell, everything I have is from you. And, you've got the power to take it all away. This situation seriously sucks but I'm still on Team God & will continue to worship you & praise your name.

Job 1:20-21 LOLV

Interpretation:
We've all been there, on the receiving end of a horrible situation or some seriously icky news, but at the end of the day what matters more than anything - is our faith. Now, I'm pretty sure I can say with confidence that even some of our worst days have come no where near close to what Job experienced, and still, he was able to maintain faith in God, that he was still in control, and had a method to his madness.

Prayer:
Dear Heavenly Father, Please help to strengthen my faith. I never want to doubt or question you, and at times that can feel hard. But I know you are in control and have a plan for everything, In your name. Amen.

Reflection:

Reflect back on some of the more trying days, situations, or experiences you've had in life. Now, think about how God has proven time and time again that he's always there beside us, supporting us through even the darkest days. Knowing he's there, will always be there, that's faith ladies.

 Strength

Sisters, those who trust in the Lord will find renewed strength. They'll soar like eagles, run without weariness, and walk without fainting.

Job 1:20-21 LOLV

Interpretation:

When I first started running half-marathons, this was the verse that kept me going. It wasn't easy running 3.1 miles in the sticky Florida heat, but I didn't let it get me down because I knew that my trust in the Lord would provide me with the strength I needed to accomplish my goals. We're made to soar, like the eagles. We do not get weary, sure, we may get body tired, but with God, we'll always have the energy needed to go on. We walk confidently, knowing that our strength comes from a source larger than ourselves.

Prayer:

Jesus, I love how you see us not only as your children, but as eagles. You place us in the world to soar high, to watch over others. You renew my strength whenever I begin to feel faint. Please give me that strength today. In your name. Amen.

Reflection:

Ladies, those who trust in the Lord experience renewed strength. That means he refills our cup anytime he starts to see us getting tired. What does this mean to you? Do you truly believe that God will renew you, living your life knowing that he's always there to support you as you move forward, or do you still hesitate, letting the world overshadow the power of God, and the strength he gives you?

 *Confidence*

Be strong. Be bold. Be confident. And fear not because you're never truly alone, no matter how quiet or dark it may seem, God is always with you.

Deuteronomy 31:7-8 LOLV

Interpretation:
Can I be real for a second? Everything that this verse says, I didn't believe. All I had for the longest time was fear. Fear of failure, fear of never being enough, fear of being too much. It took a long time for me to start feeling confident and it's something I'm still working on, every single day. I use affirmations every morning, and again throughout the day if I feel my confidence shaking, or my stress levels going up. But now, as I start to embrace my confidence and feel it more genuinely, other people are beginning to see it too. They're recognizing me for what I'm doing, the message I'm sharing, and the confidence I possess because of God and the magic he's working through me.

Prayer:
Dear Heavenly Father, On the days when I'm feeling less confident, thank you for allowing me to lean on you. Thank you for reminding me of the faith you have in me, and reminding me that I've been created in your image on purpose, with a purpose. In your name. Amen.

Reflection:

Where in your life do you feel most confident? Where do you feel least confident? What actions can you take to better embrace that confidence and shake any fear that may creep in?

 *Savior*

God is my homeboy, my backup, my cheerleader, my trainer, mentor, and savior. I've no reason to fear earthquakes, tsunamis, hurricanes, or crowds of squealing teens, because I know he's always watching out.

Psalm 46:1-3 LOLV

Interpretation:
Nowadays it seems like we're always being watched, whether we like it or not. But, one thing we can always smile about is that our Father above is keeping an eye on things. He knows not only what we're currently doing, but has a clear vision of our path into the future, even with the twists and turns we may throw in with our daily choices.

Prayer:
Dear Heavenly Father, Thank you for loving me, for supporting me, and for always protecting me against the evils of the world. I believe that you are the only reason I'm alive today, and I desire to live my life in a way that gives glory to you. In your name. Amen.

Reflection:

Have you accepted God into your heart to be your ultimate bodyguard? Why not? What's holding you back? If you're worried about your sins or mistakes, don't! They're gone. Of course, he'd love for us to try our best to not keep sinning, but he understands that mistakes happen, and he loves us no matter what. How is your relationship with God? What actions can you take today to strengthen that connection and allow him even more into your life than he is right now?

 # Challenges

Those who have faith in the Lord their God will face challenges without fear. Their hearts are unshaken, established, and filled with love.

Psalm 112:6-8 LOLV

Interpretation:
When we place our faith and trust in God, we're better prepared to face some pretty big challenges with resilience and courage, instead of being overwhelmed and shaking with fear. Sure, we're still going to experience some scary things in life, but with God on our side, we never have to do it alone.

Prayer:
Dear Heavenly Father, Please continue to fill me with your love that I might strengthen my faith in you and face any challenges that come my way without fear or hesitation. In your name. Amen.

Reflection:

What are you afraid of? What experiences or situations in life give you pause or hesitation? Have you shared these things with God?

 *Peace*

Time to hustle for peace and build each other up!

Romans 14:19 LOLV

Interpretation:
Did you think that you weren't going to have to work for peace? That it was just some free gift that came with being alive? The Romans were a people that truly had to fight for their peace so that they could build themselves up. That's exactly how God is, he's asking that we put in just the smallest bit of effort every day, and he'll take care of the rest. The more you hustle and help others, the quicker you'll experience your own peace and understanding.

Prayer:
Dear Heavenly Father. Now is my time. I don't know what I've done in the past, or why, however, I know that moving forward, I desire peace in my life and I'm willing to do what it takes to make that happen with your support and guidance. In your name. Amen

Reflection:

What do you think about when you hear the word hustle? What comes to mind? Is it a bad thing or a good thing? Maybe a mix of both? How about when you think about hustling for peace - not so bad right? What does hustling mean to you, in your daily life? Now is the time to make those little moves towards a life of peace.

 *Shine*

Dear hearts, don't grow weary of doing good. In due season, you'll reap a harvest if you don't give up. Keep shining, and keep sowing those seeds of love.

Galatians 6:9 LOLV

Interpretation:
Did you know that you're a beacon of light? Seriously. You being you, exactly as God created you. Sure, life can be difficult. We all know it. But it's what you do, how you act, carry yourself, when life isn't roses that shows the world who you really are. It's those moments when God is shining through you, for others to see, to gain inspiration, and to believe that they too are worthy of shining.

Prayer:
Dear Heavenly Father, Thank you for allowing my heart to never grow weary when things are more difficult. Thank you for creating me with my own unique shine and for giving me countless opportunities every day to share my light with others. In your name. Amen.

Reflection:

When do you feel like you shine the most? What things, experience, situations in life make you want to shine? What shine do you notice and appreciate most in others? How can you shine a little brighter today, and on days where you find yourself tempted to hide?

 *Breathe*

Hey fam, listen up! Quick tip: be speedy to hear each other out, take your sweet time before you talk, and chill before you go all Hulk-mode angry.

James 1:19 LOLV

Interpretation:
When you feel yourself getting upset, frustrated, angry, or overwhelmed. Stop. Breathe. And instead of acting quickly from a negative place, let yourself take a moment to process what you're feeling. What's happening. Then, and only then, take action. Trust me, it's a lot easier to apologize for taking a break than it is from destroying a building!

Prayer:
Dear Lord, Thank you for allowing me the time I need to process my emotions, in order to avoid lashing out or saying things I may regret. In your name. Amen.

Reflection:

How do you usually react in times of stress? Are you someone who acts first and thinks later? How might you be able to better remind yourself to pause, breathe, and act only once you've had a chance to think things through?

 *Words*

Keep the chat graceful, sprinkle in some salty wisdom. That way, you'll always have the perfect comeback, no matter who's in the conversation.

Colossians 4:6 LOLV

Interpretation:
Have you ever heard a lady in the South say, "Bless your heart?" We all know she's saying something else, but hiding it behind much nicer words. Our words carry power with them, and are impossible to take back once spoken aloud. It's like our mother's always said, "If you don't have anything nice to say, don't say anything at all."

Prayer:
Lord, help me to watch my tongue as I speak. Please help me to remember that words are not just words, and allow my words to show grace to myself and others. In your name. Amen.

Reflection:

Have you ever thought about the words you use regularly? How do you talk about others when they aren't present? How do you talk about yourself? In what ways can you better focus the words you use on the positive, the silver linings in life, and less on the negative or demeaning?

 *Worries*

Unload all your worries onto God, because he cares about you, sis.

1 Peter 5:7 LOLV

Interpretation:

Why are you worrying? God is never, ever, ever, ever going to leave you alone. He will never give us more than we can handle. What good is worrying doing you? Aside from bringing added stress, frustration, headaches, sleepless nights, and ulcers. Instead, live your life, with the comfort of knowing that God loves you, protects you, and will never let you down.

Prayer:

Dear Heavenly Father, thank you so much for showing me how your love breaks down all of the worries I have, or could ever have. Whatever happens, I know that this too shall pass. In your name. Amen.

Reflection:

What things are you worrying about, today, right now? Are they things you can resolve, or accept as an unknown and move along? Do you take these worries to God? Trust me, he wants to hear the things that are on your mind and your heart. He wants to help carry those for you, to soothe those worries, and give you peace.

 *Discipline*

Hun, discipline stings for a bit, but trust me, it grows into a peaceful fruit of righteousness. So, stand tall, strengthen those weak spots, and keep your path straight. Strive for peace with everyone, and chase after holiness to catch a glimpse of the Lord.

Hebrews 12:11-14 LOLV

Interpretation:
Discipline hurts. Anyone who had a rebellious streak as a child can attest to that. But, the more and more we do as we're meant to, the more we trust, that sting happens less and less. So queens, lift up your crowns. Straighten them up. Work on the weak spots but know that you're going in the right direction. Keep it up. You're doing amazing. And remember, we all wander off track sometimes. We're human after all.

Prayer:
Lord, Thank you for creating me as such a strong, powerful, unique woman. I know I may wander at times, but I also know that you love me, no matter what. Thank you for always helping to steer me in the right direction and never leaving me alone. In your name. Amen.

Reflection:

Where are your weak spots? The places where you find yourself wandering, and needing God's pull back to the right path? We all have them, so stop judging yourself for your imperfections. God never gives up on us, he's the epitome of giving second chances. What can you do to strengthen your weak spots?

 *Reward*

God whispered, 'Don't be scared, my dear. I've got your back, and your reward? It's gonna be epic.

Genesis 15:1 LOLV

Interpretation:
Tell me, do you love getting a reward? I know I do! The rewards that God gives us are bigger than the most outrageous impossible dream you could ever imagine. You know what that means? Everything we do in life, it's worth it. Even the really hard stuff.

Prayer:
Dear Father, Please help me to keep my eyes and ears open for the signs and rewards you provide. And continue to help me be patient and understand that everything happens in your divine timing. In your name. Amen.

Reflection:

What type of signs are you asking God for? Mine have always been blue butterflies. When I'm overwhelmed or confused about something in life, I'll take it to God in a prayer, and before I know it, sure enough, I'll see a little blue butterfly flitting by. Now, God doesn't always answer us when we want him to, or how we want him to, but what matters is that you're sharing your life with him, and trusting that when the time is right, he'll let you know.

 *Breathe*

Chill, don't stress about tomorrow, darling. Tomorrow can handle its own worries. Today has enough on its plate.

Matthew 6:34 LOLV

Interpretation:
God did us a solid, creating night as a time each and every day, when we can rest He knew that our days would be absolutely filled with obligations, projects, work, family, friends, grocery shopping, laundry. So, he gave us night, a chance to breathe, to relax, to settle back and reflect on what we've accomplished, how remarkable the world around us is, and giving thanks for the blessings we've received. Worrying about tomorrow doesn't serve anyone, and God knows that. So, breathe. Really, breathe.

Prayer:
Dear Lord, Thank you for creating a life with plenty of time to breathe and rest. Thank you for never giving me more than I can handle, and for always being by my side cheering me on. In your name. Amen.

Reflection:

When was the last time you really sat back, kicked up your feet, rested, and breathed? Sure, we take breaks when we're ready to break, when we've driven ourselves to the end of our rope. But, do you breathe before then? Set an alarm or appointment for yourself, 10 minutes every day, when you can step away from technology, close your eyes, and breathe.

 *Level*

Ladies, listen up. If you can't keep your cool, it's like a city without walls – vulnerable and wide open. Guard your heart, queens.

Proverbs 25:28 LOLV

Interpretation:

It can be hard sometimes, dealing with different types of people and interactions while trying to stay levelheaded. When we're able to remain calm, it helps our entire body to stay balanced, keeping us from moving into fight or flight mode, and better guarding ourselves against the threat of harm from both physical and unseen forces. One thing is for sure though, blowing up or lashing out always causes more harm than good. So the next time you find yourself fighting the world, struggling to stay calm, take a deep breath, press pause, and pray. God is always listening.

Prayer:

Dear Heavenly Father, Please bless me in all interactions I have today. I know that each of us are going through our own experiences and it can be a trial to keep our cool. Please help me to remain open and understanding to those around me. In your name. Amen.

Reflection:

Are you someone that's able to stay calm and levelheaded in stressful situations, or do you find yourself flying off the handle and lashing out? What can you do to better guard your heart while remaining open and understanding to those around you who may be dealing with things they aren't yet equipped to handle?

 *Forgiveness*

Ladies, forgiveness nurtures friendship, while dwelling on disputes pushes friends away.

Proverbs 17:9 LOLV

Interpretation:
Have you ever had an argument completely ruin a friendship? We've all been there, and often, after the fact, we realize that the issue that came between us, was something minor and in the grand scheme of things, not worth it. By listening, instead of dwelling on who was right or wrong, we're able to give those friendships a chance to mend and strengthen.

Prayer:
Dear God, Please nurture my friendships, those I have now as well as those that may have been strained in the past. Please help me to show forgiveness over anger. In your name. Amen.

Reflection:

Think back to a close friendship you used to have, but have lost due to an argument or misunderstanding. Is this something you experience often in life? How might you be able to better approach these relationships from a place of forgiveness and understanding in the future?

 # Trustworthy

Here's the deal boo. When it comes to God's mysteries, you gotta be a trustworthy steward. Keep the faith, stay true.

1 Corinthians 4:2 LOLV

Interpretation:
Sure, this may sound a bit like the chicken and the egg conundrum. But at the end of the day, God needs us to trust him as much as he trusts us. The gifts he's given us, the amazing amount of power and trust that he's placed in us, his children, to help share his message through our words and our actions, it's pretty phenomenal when you think about it.

Prayer:
Dear Heavenly Father, Please help me to shake off the negativity of the world around me. I appreciate the trust you've placed in me, and I'm going to do my best today and every day, to be deserving of that trust. In your name. Amen.

Reflection:

Do you trust God? Do you trust yourself? Do you trust others in your life? What does being trustworthy mean to you? Is it based on actions or words? How might you be able to become a more trustworthy person? How can you better trust others?

 # Adoration

God cares for you more than ever. He remembers how you all followed him, showering him with love, respect, and a touch of awe.

2 Corinthians 7:15 LOLV

Interpretation:
When you think about it, God really is the biggest celebrity any of us could hope to connect with. And, we're blessed because he's chosen us to be in his elite group of friends, followers, disciples. He adores us as much if not more than we adore him, and really, who doesn't dream of that kind of a relationship?

Prayer:
Dear Lord, Thank you for choosing me, not only as one of your children, but every single day of my life. Thank. you for showing me your love and allowing me to love you in the best ways I know how. In your name. Amen.

Reflection:

How do you show your adoration for God? Is it in your words, your actions, or the ways in which you treat others?

Insight

Let me spill some wisdom, ladies. People might chase after empty dreams, but our God is the real deal. His love and promises? Timeless and everlasting. Don't get tangled up in the wrong stuff.

Jeremiah 16:20-11 LOLV

Interpretation:
Whose dreams are you chasing after? Are they yours, something you saw on TV, or are you chasing the dreams God has for you? His love and promises are timeless and everlasting, and as Jeremiah said, "Don't get tangled up in earthly issues." God will never lead you astray and leave your life in disarray. Spoiler: God is and always will be chasing us, while we're busy chasing earthy things.

Prayer:
Thank you, Father for chasing after me, even when I chase after the dreams that you don't have planned for me. Your love, your promises, and your everlasting wisdom is all I really need. In your name. Amen.

Reflection:

Did you know that God's love promises everlasting grace, and it's all sitting there waiting for us? If you knew that you could achieve anything, what would you tell your younger self?

 *Gratitude*

Sweet souls, don't let worries take over. Pour out your heart to God with gratitude, and His peace, beyond understanding, will be your fortress through Christ Jesus

Philippians 4:6-7 LOLV

Interpretation:
I am in awe every single day of the gratitude that God shows me. Which sounds a little crazy, I know. When I'm talking to God, no matter what words I'm choosing to use, or where I'm at, I know he's listening, and grateful that I'm taking the time to share my life, my thoughts, and my excitement, with him. While I'm grateful for everything God has done, and continues to do for me every day, I know that he's just as grateful for me.

Prayer:
Dear Heavenly Father, I know the path that I want to walk down may not always be the one you've chosen and set forth for me. I'm so grateful that you allow me to make my own decisions, and with that my own mistakes, and for never leaving me no matter what I do. In your name. Amen.

Reflection:

What's holding you back from God's fortress? Do you not believe that you're worthy? That you haven't completed the list of requirements? Maybe you feel like you haven't been grateful enough for the gifts God has given you. Instead, try having a quick conversation with God - let him know what you're thinking and feeling.

 *Purpose*

Here's the essence of life – honor God and keep His commandments. It's the real deal, the whole purpose of our journey.

Ecclesiastes 12:13-14 LOLL

Interpretation:

I know we've all wondered what our purpose is in life. Whether it's with our job, our relationships, our family - what is our purpose? That's easy ladies. Our purpose is to follow the commandments set out by God. That's it. Easy, right? Sure, some of those commandments seem a little wordy & outdated, but I think we can all agree that the golden rule encompasses them all, and stands true today. God brought us here to experience the journey of life. To honor the rules he set out for us, to love one another, and to be a good person. A sister, a mother, a daughter, an aunt, a friend.

Prayer:

God, you know I've questioned my purpose from time to time, sometimes out loud and others in my own thoughts. As I go through today, this week, this month, please continue to provide me with direction on living my purpose, as an essential part of your plan. In your name. Amen.

Reflection:

How are you living your purpose today? What have you thought of as your life purpose, in the past? How has it changed? Are you currently living your life purpose for God or man?

 *Design*

Sister, you have been crafted with love and purpose. Your life is a unique work of art, designed to shine.

Ephesians 2:10 LOLV

Interpretation:
We have not been designed to fail. Nothing about you is a flaw or failure in God's plan. Each and every one of us has been designed, to the most minute detail. Period.

Prayer:
Dear Lord, Thank you for creating me just as I am, just as you've chosen. There are times where I feel like I may not be sparkling as much as I could, but I know you have a plan designed for me. In your name. Amen.

Reflection:

What are some of the unique traits you possess? Try and list 20 of them. Trust me, there are far more than that. You've been designed by God, uniquely and perfectly as you are.

Listen up, beautiful babes. I spilled the tea so you can have my kind of peace. Yeah, there'll be tough times in this world, but keep your chin up. I've conquered it all.

John 16:33 LOLV

Interpretation:
As a Southerner, we love our sweet tea. But nothing comes close to the tea God shares through his messages in the Bible, as well as in the way he's created us in his image, providing us with the peace that only comes from knowing we are the children of God.

Prayer:
Dear Lord, Thanks for spilling your tea, conquering the world, and always being here when I need you. I'm forever grateful to you for the peace you provide me every day. In. your name. Amen.

Reflection:

God wants us to know his peace, and a part of that is being able to share our worries, our struggles, our pain, our frustrations, and our celebrations with him. How do you feel most comfortable communicating with God?

 *Duty*

Beloved friends, since God showered us with His immense love, let's make it our duty to love one another.

1 John 4:11 LOLV

Interpretation:
All you have to do is turn on the news. Click on SnapChat, Facebook, X, and you see nothing but hatred, anger, and violence. That's not what God wants for us. He doesn't want us fighting to death, to prove to him and the world that we're the best. The most powerful. He didn't create us to fight or be violent. He created us in HIS image, showering us with the commitment that all we have to do is love each other. All he wants for us is to love. To experience love. Love that comes from our soul, deep inside at our core. Now, we may not like some people, we are human after all. But, when we really think about it, the times we struggle with loving, often stem from misunderstanding. So, remember, even when we don't exactly understand someone or where they're coming from, that it's okay. God never said we have to understand everyone, just that we should love them. Like he loves us. All of us.

Prayer:
Lord, I give you my heart and my love, to show others with every step I take, the love you have for them, through me. I give you my body, to shine bright and share your word. In your name. Amen.

Reflection:

Like John says, let's make it out duty to love one another. What do you love about yourself? Often we find it most difficult to love who we are. How do you feel when other people compliment you, showing you love with their words and appreciation? How can you show love for one person today?

Smile

May the words from my lips and the thoughts in my heart make You smile, O Lord, my Rock and my Redeemer. Your approval means everything.

Psalm 19:14 LOLV

Interpretation:
Personally, when I'm having a hard time, I share my thoughts out loud with God. I recenter, find something to laugh about, or a good song to jam out to. At the end of it all, I smile, because I'm alive. Then, I thank God. Lather. Rinse. Repeat. We're safe with God. He's out protector, so no matter what it is that's going on in our lives around us, the best we can do is keep the line of communication open, and smile. And, at the end of the day, the more smile and laugh lines we have on our faces, the more amazing our life has been.

Prayer:
Lord, thank you for blessing me with another day where I can smile. When others see my smile, allow it to light their life up in some small way. My purpose here is to connect with others, and to share your joy. In your name. Amen.

Reflection:

When was the last time you enjoyed a moment, watched the world pass by, and smiled? When was the last time you laughed out loud? Not just typed 'lol' in a text message to a friend, but open mouthed, eyes closed, belly laughed? Life is too short. Smile and laugh as often as possible.

Desire

Hey, queens, delight in the Lord, and let Him shape your desires. Trust Him with your journey, and watch your path unfold in His radiant light.

Psalm 37:4-6 LQLV

Interpretation:
The first time I read this verse I was hoping it meant that God was going to shape my body the way I wanted it to be - sadly, not so much. What it does mean is that God is helping to shape the desires we have. We get to allow God to help show us the path, the plan he has for us, and while we still have countless choices in our journey, he's always there beside us to help us move in the right direction, to desire the things that are best for us, and for our relationship with him.

Prayer:
Dear Heavenly Father, Thank you for making me the queen I am. I know that at times the things I desire are material and earthly, but above all, I desire to be closer to you, to fulfill the plans you have set out for me. In your name. Amen.

Reflection:

What are the things you find yourself desiring most in life? Are they experiences, material items, people, or relationships? How do you feel when you achieve or obtain these desires? How do you think you might feel if what you desired most was a stronger relationship with God? What actions can you take today, to move towards that all-important desire?

 *Pain*

Job screamed out in pain, like he was being pricked with a million dull needles, because he basically was. "God, this really really REALLY sucks! Why didn't you just kill me before I was born? I'd rather not have lived at all if this is what my life is going to be. Seriously, every part of my mind, body, and spirit are suffering right now and I'm pretty sure the light I see at the end of the tunnel, is a train.

Job 3:11-26 LOLV

Interpretation:
Anyone who's experienced physical pain understands that it's no joke. Not only can it be difficult to move your body, but to breathe, and sometimes, even thinking feels impossible. This is what Job was dealing with. But, even while he was screaming at God, begging to be put out of his misery, he never gave up on the fact that God had a plan for him. Even in our darkest hours, we get to take those worries, fears, frustrations to God and ask that he give us the strength to keep going. Remember, God will never leave us alone.

Prayer:
Dear Lord, My physical body isn't as strong as I wish it were, and sometimes it hurts to move or breathe. Please continue to give me the strength I need, to stay faithful, to keep trusting in you and your plan. In your name. Amen.

Reflection:

Think about a time in life when you've been in pain physically. Did you give up or did you try to stay strong, to heal and regain your ability to move? God never gives us more than we can handle, and it's up to us to communicate with him, when we need his help and guidance. He loves us and doesn't want to see us suffer.

 Plans

Ladies, God's plans are unstoppable, and no one can thwart His awesome schemes. Rock on!

Job 42:2 LOLV

Interpretation:
When God puts his mind to something, there's nothing and no one that can stop him. His plans for you are great, they're unique, and he created them especially for you, no one else. Feels pretty amazing doesn't it?

Prayer:
Dear God, Thank you for creating me as I am and for being such a compassionate and protective savior. I wake up every morning, filled with excitement to pursue the plans you have for me. In your name. Amen.

Reflection:

Have you experienced times in life when the plans you made seemed to bump up against the plans God has for you? How have you realized this? Was it a feeling? A whisper? A message you received?

 *Trust*

Soul sisters, fear not! God is with you, holding your hand and giving you strength. So, gorgeous, don't be anxious; trust, trust, trust.

Isaiah 41:10 LOLV

Interpretation:
As a child, being adopted, trust was not a word that was in my vocabulary. I didn't know what trust was. I feared so much in life and was constantly overwhelmed and anxious when it came to the idea of trusting anyone, including my parents, and God. But, my grandmother, she feared not and trusted the Lord fully. She offered me the opportunity to be baptized, as a means of showing me that someone, God, would always be there to guide me. That I was always loved. No questions asked.

Prayer:
Lord, Please protect the souls on this Earth. Reach out your hand and give them strength when they are anxious. Give them a hug and show them that you're always there for them. That they can trust you fully, put down their walls, and know that you are King. In your name. Amen.

Reflection:

Do you trust God, your family, your friends, yourself? Why or why not? If not, what is it that you fear? There's only one relationship in our lives that we can fully trust, and that's with our Lord. He's always beside us, holding our hand, giving us strength, and cheering us on, no matter what.

 *Mortality*

Sis, life is fleeting. What mortal lasts forever? Show me a lady who doesn't face life's clock ticking away. None, right?

Psalm 89:48 LOLV

Interpretation:
As humans, we don't have magic wands to turn back the hands of the clock. We have one life, with many chapters. While it makes sense that we want to remain young for as long as possible, it's important that we remember, the present, our life, in this moment, is what we get to focus on most. The events of yesterday don't have to rule how we live today. Every morning we wake up, God is giving us a new opportunity.

Prayer:
Dear God, in this fleeting life, please help me to live in the present moment. Please fill my days with the plans you've outlined for me. In your name. Amen.

Reflection:

When you think about your life, what do you want to accomplish or achieve most? How do you want to be remembered? How can you better set out to live every single day of your life with passion and appreciation?

 *Comfort*

Cry out when you need to and the Lord will hear you, rescuing you from even the craziest of situations. He is never far from the broken-hearted.

Psalm 34:17-19 LOLV

Interpretation:
When was the last time you hid in your bathroom crying over something that seemed life-threatening at the time, but after a few hours, days, weeks, wound up being nothing worse than a little spilled milk? Yea, me too. When we have those moments, God doesn't want us to suffer alone. He doesn't want us to hide away in shame, he wants us to cry out to him. He begs us to share with him what's going on in our lives so that he can be a part of the solution, of making us feel better. Trust me girlfriend. God has the best shoulder to cry on, and is an amazing listener.

Prayer:
Dear Lord, thank you for always listening to me. Even when it feels like the things I'm sharing with you might be silly or petty, you always listen. Thank you for never judging me or making me feel like any less of a woman for the human things I experience. In your name. Amen.

Reflection:

Alright friend, set a timer for 10-minutes and make a list below of all of the things that are currently bothering you. What's worrying you, annoying you, frustrating you? Are you feeling heartbroken? Alone? Scared? Share it all with God. Trust me, he's always listening.

 *Connection*

Facts are facts: Nothing – not death, life, angels, or any other circumstance – can separate us from the love of God.

Romans 8:38-39 LOLV

Interpretation:
If you know nothing about my life, know this, I've died. A few times in fact. The connections that I've formed with the people closest to me, as well as my connection with God, have carried me throughout every day since I woke up in that sterile hospital bed. Even on the days when we feel most alone, forgotten, or misunderstood, God maintains his connection with us. He's always there, waiting with his arms outstretched, waiting for us to embrace him.

Prayer:
Dear Heavenly Father, Thank you for the unfaltering love and connection you show me on a daily basis. Thank you for always being there, waiting for me, seeing me, supporting me, through the struggles of my daily life. In your name. Amen.

Reflection:

When is a time or situation when you've found yourself feeling most alone and without connection, to friends, family, yourself? When have you felt the strongest connections in life?

 # Righteousness

Queens, wisdom from above is crystal clear, peaceable, gentle, and open-minded. Packed with mercy and good vibes, it's impartial and real. Plant seeds of righteousness in peace, and watch a harvest bloom.

James 3:17-18 LQLV

Interpretation:

After writing and publishing my first book, the question everyone asked was, "How do you feel?" They thought when my book was finished and available for people to read, I would be excited, and that when I was able to hold it in my own hands, everything would change. But what truly excited me was hearing and seeing people talking about my book, the stories I'd shared, the messages from God that I'd been able to communicate to others. I didn't know it at the time but deciding to write a book, that was God working through me. It was a part of the path he laid out for me, to become the woman I am today, in full bloom. All we have to do is keep an open mind, ears, and heart, trusting that God is righteous and working through us.

Prayer:

Dear Heavenly Father, Allow my work today to be impacted by listening to and living in your righteousness. Please continue to share your wisdom, openmindedness, mercy, and good vibes with me, and through me. I'm doing my best to stand in peace, patiently watching the seeds you're planting today, as they bloom fully. In your name. Amen.

Reflection:

Where in your life are you living with an open mind? Are you staying open to the whispers of God? The wisdom he's providing you with every single day? Or, are you closed off, living life on your terms? How can you open yourself up to better watch the seeds God is planting in your life as they glow and bloom?

# Compassion

Sisters, as God's chosen, holy, and dearly loved, let's dress ourselves in compassion, kindness, humility, gentleness, and patience. Hold each other close and forgive freely, just as the Lord forgave you. And above all, let's wrap ourselves in the exquisite garment of love, the bond that unites us in perfect unity.

Colossians 3:12-14 LOLV

Interpretation:
How amazing does it feel when you try on the perfect pair of jeans or that fun summer dress complete with pockets? Well ladies, I've got news for you. Multiply that feeling by a million and you'll begin to understand how it feels when we wrap ourselves in the love of God. Trust me, not even a dress with pockets compares to the compassion, kindness, and patience our Lord has for us - and the best part, he's always got our perfect size.

Prayer:
Dear Lord, thank you for always taking care of me, showing me love, kindness, and compassion, even when I'm feeling unlovable. Your patience is a reminder that I'm your child, and you'll never leave me alone. In your name. Amen.

Reflection:

When was the last time you asked for forgiveness? How did it feel, when you handed over any guilt or shame and accepted God's undying love in return? Are there any people in your life that you need to forgive or ask forgiveness from? What steps can you take this week, to show love, patience, and forgiveness for others, the way our Lord does for us?

Grace

Soul sisters, above all, let's love each other deeply; love covers a multitude of sins. Embrace hospitality without grumbling, and let's use our unique gifts to serve one another, being the stewards of God's incredible grace.

1 Peter 4:8-10 LOLV

Interpretation:
Grace is an idea that gets thrown around in the world in many different ways. What God is talking about here is the grace that's given to you by him, it was designed just for you. Not anyone else. Jesus knew that we were still going to sin, even after he'd given his life for us. He knew that each and every one of us had a gift that needed to be served. The only way that your gifts are truly served is by having grace for others, as well as by showing yourself grace. Allow yourself the time, space, and grace to access, embrace, and authentically share those gifts.

Prayer:
Dear Heavenly Father, thank you for giving me grace in a world that's full of sin. I want to be a steward of your message, and I understand that learning grace is the first step in that journey. In your name. Amen.

Reflection:

What does love mean to you? We've all heard of the different love languages, what's yours? Do you find yourself seeking love from other people, from animals, from family, friends? I've got a secret for you, the love we receive from our Heavenly Father is a million times bigger than any other love we can ever experience. So, embrace your unique gifts today, show yourself grace, and love yourself. How can you show yourself a little more grace today?

 *Doors*

Beloved, faith is your superpower. When you seek God, believing in His goodness, He throws open the doors and showers you with His love.

Hebrews 11:6 LOLV

Interpretation:
We were all born with a superpower. God saw to that. Figuring out what that power is though can require faith, a lot of faith. Some of us recognize these powers right away, others, it takes a little while longer. However, Faith is one superpower that God provided to all of his children. Having faith in God is like walking outside into the sun, feeling the warmth of the rays covering every inch of your body. This is what God's love feels like, when we fully trust and have faith in his goodness, his mercy, his unwavering belief in us.

Prayer:
Hey God, Thank you for always opening doors and showering me with love, even when my faith seems weak. Thank you for allowing me to have my own superpowers, and showing me where I can use those to support and encourage others. In your name. Amen.

Reflection:

What's your superpower? Be honest here, brag a little. Chances are you've got more than one, and definitely more than you realize. Ask the people who love you most, what they see as being your areas of expertise. How can you better lean into your faith and other superpowers today? God gave them to you for a reason. He's waiting for you to open the door.

Authority

Queens, gather 'round! Jesus spilled the tea – all authority is in his hands. Go, make disciples, and spread the love. It's your mission!

Matthew 28:18-20 LOLV

Interpretation:

This one's easy my friends. God's love is amazing and he wants us to share it with everyone. Your mom, your sister, your colleagues, your friends, the lady you see at the grocery store! Sharing is caring and God's message is the biggest CARE we can give to others. So, what are you waiting for?

Prayer:

Dear Lord, Please use me as a vessel to spread your message, your love, your compassion, and your grace to everyone I meet today. In your name. Amen.

Reflection:

When was the last time you shared about the word of God with someone? Not in a preachy way, but simply sharing the good news that God loves THEM, sent his son to die for them, to save them, to provide them with eternal life in heaven.

 *Strategy*

Sweetheart, listen up! God made everything with a purpose, even the wicked for judgment day. He's the master strategist.

Proverbs 16:4 LOLV

Interpretation:
Hey, are you good at playing Tetris or packing the car before a big trip? Imagine being God - strategically planning the perfect design for each and every one of his children, our lives, and our families. And he did so, not by looking for the little spaces where he could cram an extra pillow or can of beans, but instead, created space to allow for everything we'll ever need on our journey through life.

Prayer:
Dear Heavenly Father. Thank you for setting up my life in the way you have. I've forever thankful for the ways in which you've designed and organized my life in a way that best serves you. In your name. Amen.

Reflection:

Do you have a strategy for how you live your life? Do you tackle the easiest tasks first, putting off those that seem a little more daunting for later? Or, do you trust that God has a divine plan for you, and your life? How can you better hand over the reins to God when it comes to the strategy of your life?

 *Wisdom*

Hey, ladies with deep hearts, wisdom's like a door. Search it out, it's worth the knock.

Proverbs 20:5 LOLV

Interpretation:
Knock Knock. Did you hear that? It's the door of wisdom. We've all heard the phrase, "respect your elders," well, we should be listening to them as well. Wisdom has little to do with age and much to do with lived experience. Wisdom is a gift offered to us by God, in the lessons he teaches us, the people he brings into our lives, and the love he shows us each and every day. When we bring our questions, our troubles, our issues to him, he opens that door, and shines a light of patience, understanding, and wisdom, allowing us to see a clear path through the storm.

Prayer:
Thank you Father for always having an open door, anytime I may need your expert advice and wisdom. In your name. Amen.

Reflection:

When was the last time you knocked on God's door? Or do you find yourself seeking help and guidance from your fellow woman? Where does your wisdom come from? Reliable sources pr people who really just want to hear themselves talk? Knowing that God is the keeper of wisdom and clarity, how can you better take your questions to him and trust the guidance he provides?

 *Joy*

Perfume and incense bring joy to the heart, just like the delightful advice from a true friend.

Proverbs 27:9 LOLV

Interpretation:
God is the truest of friends. Embracing his message, his advice to us, in the gospels fills our lives with pure joy. Everything in our lives that we have, that we receive, is proof of this.

Prayer:
Lord, May others see in my actions that I believe in your son Jesus because of the joy that flows from me. Thank you for providing your word as a constant source of advice and direction. In your name. Amen.

Reflection:
Do you consider God to be a friend? Do you talk to him like you do a friend? Do you share your excitements, celebrations, worries, and hesitations with him the way you do your closest of girlfriends? Believe it or not, he wants to hear it.

 *Trust*

Trust the Lord wholeheartedly; don't rely on your own understanding. In every step, acknowledge him, and he'll guide your path.

Proverbs 3:5-6 LOLV

Interpretation:
You think you have the answers or know what your next steps are going to be? Every time we try to do something our way it may work out for a little bit but then eventually come crashing down. That's what comes from being a control freak. Instead, talk with God daily and let him know your thoughts. Give these things to him, to do with as he's planned, and trust that he's got your best interests in mind.

Prayer:
Lord, trusting is hard but I'm aware that without trusting you I'll continue experiencing mistakes from my own misguided actions. I give you my trust, even if I do try to take it back from time to time. I know you love me, and understand that I'm trying my best. I love you God. Amen.

Reflection:

When you think of the word trust what comes to mind? Is it easy for you to trust or do you clam up tightly, so no one will ever see the pearl you're hiding inside? What parts of your life can you release in the hands of God? Know and trust that he will never forsake you.

Weakness

I find joy in my vulnerabilities and the struggles, insults, and trials that come my way for Christ's sake. Because in my weakness, I discover strength.

2 Corinthians 12:10 LOLV

Interpretation:
Weakness is one of the best attributes we can possess because it allows us the chance to discover the full magnitude of our power. By embracing our struggles, we're able to strengthen our mind, body, and soul. We're stronger than we ever thought we might be, and you never know what silver linings we'll discover when we remain open to the areas where we can improve our lives.

Prayer:
Dear Heavenly Father. Please allow my fellow sisters to find joy and understanding within their weaknesses, coming to terms with their struggles and vulnerabilities. Show them their unique strengths as they walk through their daily life. In your name. Amen.

Reflection:

Do you consider yourself to be strong? Are there areas in life where you sometimes see yourself as being an underdog? There areas of weakness are opportunities for us to ask God to come into our lives, filling us with his wisdom, clarity, and strength, so that we might grow not only in ourselves, but to be a shining light for others.

 *Hope*

Girlfriend, God's got big plans for you – plans filled with hope and a bright future. Trust the journey, it's going to be amazing.

Jeremiah 29:11 LOLV

Interpretation:
God designed YOU, yes YOU, to be a bright shining star to light the path for the journey he has planned for you. That journey may be hard, and at times, that light may seem faint, but with God by your side, the most amazing chapters of your life are yet to be written. Trust me friend, it's about to get real good!

Prayer:
Dear God. Thank you for always having hope for me. I'm going to do my best to make today amazing, shining my light for others to see, bringing a smile to the faces of others, and giving them hope, in your name. Amen.

Reflection:

What can you do today, this week, this month, this year, that will allow you to have more hope in your life? How can you shine brighter in your life, to act as a guiding light and inspiration to others?

 # Companionship

Two are better than one, sisters, for they support each other to succeed. If one falls, the other lifts her up; a warm companion in the journey. A person standing alone can be defeated, but together, we stand strong. Three are even better – a triple-braided cord that cannot easily be broken.

Ecclesiastes 4:9-12 LOLV

Interpretation:
You know that feeling when you share a secret, a surprise, or an accomplishment with your best friends? It's almost like your hearts are twisting together, providing strength and comfort that you wouldn't have on your own. The same holds true when issues come up, having that bestie who'll stand with you, beside you, makes all the difference. As women, God wants us to cherish our friendships, because that's where we find solace, support, and the joy of shared victories.

Prayer:
Dear Lord, thank you for always being the best friend a girl could ask for. Thank you also for providing me with kindred spirits, women who understand what I'm going through and remind me that I'm never alone. They and you will always have my back. In your name. Amen.

Reflection:

Who are your ride or die friends? When was the last time you thanked them, for being there when times got tough and celebrating with you when things were great? When was the last time you thanked God, for not only being an ear to listen, a shoulder to lean on, but also for providing you with such an amazing squad of friends?

Love

Queens, my command is simple: Love one another as I have loved you. There's no greater love than laying down your life for friends. And guess what? You're not just servants; you're my cherished friends. I've shared everything I learned from my Father with you.

John 15:12-15 LOLV

Interpretation:
Ladies, this isn't about laying down your life for another life. What God's saying is that because of the action he's already taken, the life he's laid down - it was done for us to feel cherished. We aren't his servants, we're his friends and family. The love he has for us, is the same love that he wants us to show to others around us.

Prayer:
Dear Heavenly Father. I know in the past that I've laid myself down for everyone, and my friends have used me as a servant. I now ask for you to help me cherish the moments and live in your love. For that love, will never harm or kill me. In your name Amen.

Reflection:

God's commandment is simple. How did love get so messed up? If it's shared the way it's meant to be, the world wouldn't be in the shape it is now. How do you show love? Do you smile at strangers? Hold open the door for others? Do you say hello, just because? What are you going to do today, to remember that you are not a servant, but a friend of God's, meant to share his love with the world.

 *Advocacy*

Sisters, let me drop some truth on you. When you stumble, know that you've got a heavenly advocate, Jesus Christ the righteous, cheering for you.

1 John 2:1 LOLV

Interpretation:
Did you hear that mic drop? I didn't for the longest time. I was stumbling through my life, trying to figure out what to do and how to do it. I had to not only become an advocate for myself, but for my family, my aging parents, all within the span of a year. I felt like I had to do it alone, but what I know now, is that Jesus is always there, cheering us on. Without this truth, sisters, we stumble and fall. But I pray that you're able to trust that Jesus is there for you too.

Prayer:
Dear Heavenly Father, Bless me for I know that I am my best advocate, but only with you by my side. Having you here, pushing me to keep going, allows me to remain steady and not stumble. Your truth keeps me in faith. In your name. Amen.

Reflection:

Bestie - who are your advocates? Are you going to keep trying to do everything on your won, or are you going to let Jesus in, to help cheer you on, hold you up, and keep your feet moving forward? How can you allow Jesus to be your advocate today?

 Suffering

Through ugly snot bubble filled sobs Job begged, "God, if you would just tell me what I did to become your target I would ask you to forgive me. Seriously, what could I have done to piss you off so bad? Have I offended you? Am I burden? You've got to tell me quick before I give into my suffering and resign myself to death.

Job 7:20-21 LOLV

Interpretation:
Job was at the lowest of lows. He still held firm to his faith in God, but at the same time was super confused and didn't understand why he was being treated the way he was. He believed that he had to have done something really, really, really bad, because he was being physically driven to the point of giving up. Despite it all, Job didn't give up on God or his faith, no matter how severe the pain was.

Prayer:
Father. Bless me today as I strive to put my faith in you above all else. I know that I don't need to be experiencing physical pain to be suffering. Please continue to protect me against any harm that comes my way. In your name. Amen.

Reflection:

Have you ever felt like God was testing you? Have you ever found yourself suffering? Physically, mentally, emotionally, or spiritually? What kept you from giving into the pain? Have you ever taken time to consider why you were in that situation? What did you learn from the experience?

 *Resilience*

Ladies, when you pass through deep waters, I've got you. When you walk through the fires of life, you won't be scorched, and the flames won't consume you. You're wrapped in my love, resilient and unbreakable.

Isaiah 43:2 LOLV

Interpretation:
God held my hand when the unthinkable happened. I lost my fiance, found out I had cancer, and by the age of 22 lived through 2 other seriously life-altering experiences. But, I'm still here to share that God will always do what he says. He will never leave us alone.

Prayer:
Dear Lord, Please continue to protect me as I go through whatever happens today. I understand that at times the process may be like making a diamond, with lots of pressure and stress, but I trust that I will come out the other side, and you will never leave me alone. In your name. Amen.

Reflection:

What experiences have you had in life that left you fearful, or questioning if you would be able to make it out alive? How have you felt the love and power of God in those most trying times? How do you feel God's love and protection on a daily basis?

Safety

Dear ones, know this in your core: Those who seek the Lord find refuge. He won't bail on you; He's the ultimate stronghold, your safe space.

Psalm 9:10 LOLV

Interpretation:
In a sea of darkness, if you are in a relationship with God, deep down, you're safe. God is and will always be our protector, along with his team of countless angels. Even when we decide to try some crazy stuff and push the boundaries, he's always there to keep us safe.

Prayer:
Lord, as I go through my day, please provide me with a safe place to be with you. I know that you're here with me, always, as I go out into the world. In your name. Amen.

Reflection:

What does being safe mean to you? Are there times in life where you doubt your safety and find yourself shaken? How can you better trust in God's protection? How might you be able to approach life differently, with confidence in God as your guardian?

 *Promise*

Ladies, God's love never quits. His promises are solid, and He's got your back. You're in safe hands.

Psalm 138:8 LOLV

Interpretation:
Pinky promises were a big thing when I was growing up. Most of us have made them, and broken them, at some point in our lives, not God though. When he makes a pinky promise, it's for keeps. You know that whatever he tells you, it's the truth. It all started with the promise he made us, sacrificing his son to die on the cross for our sins.

Prayer:
Lord, Please forgive me for any times that I've doubted you. Your promises are the real deal and I know in my heart that you've never let me down in the past. Thank you for always showing me such love and kindness. In your name. Amen.

Reflection:

How confident do you feel in God's promises? Are there places where you still feel doubt or hesitation? Have you taken those worries to him? Trust me, he wants to hear from you - whether it's giving thanks, asking forgiveness, celebrating exciting news, or asking him for clarification on something you're feeling worried about.

 *Devotion*

Remember friend, God showed his everlasting love for us when we were still sinners. Talk about faith and devotion.

Romans 5:8 LOLV

Interpretation:
God has been devoted to use since before we were even born. He was fully aware we would sin, it's why he sent his only son to earth to die for us. Jesus showed us a way to salvation through his life, his devotion to us is why we are still here today.

Prayer:
Lord, thank you for sending your son to take all the burden off of us so that we can have a true relationship with you. In your name. Amen.

Reflection:

Have you ever been devoted to something to the point where you would die for it? How do you feel, knowing this is a gift, a sacrifice, that God has given for you?

 *Labels*

Listen up, ladies! In this space, no labels matter – not Jew or Gentile, circumcised or not, barbarian, Scythian, slave, or free. Christ is everything and in everyone.

Colossians 3:11 LOLV

Interpretation:
In this world, we are labeled or request that labels be used for nearly every aspect of our lives. God doesn't care about the words we use to describe the person we are. All he sees is that we are his daughters. As a father, he understands us because he is inside each and every one of us, whether we know it or not.

Prayer:
Dear God, Please remove my worldly labels. As your daughter, the love and blessings you provide are more than enough for me. In your name. Amen.

Reflection:

What labels do you identify with? Why do you think we find ourselves so concerned with labels in our daily lives? God made us all, in his image. Do you see yourself being confident enough to let go of the labels you hold, to be the raw, real woman God made you as?

 *Value*

Ladies, take a deep breath in! Don't stress about what to wear or what's for dinner. Life's about more than that. Trust the One who clothes the lilies and feeds the birds. You're way more valuable, darling.

Matthew 6:25 LOLV

Interpretation:
Life goes at 100mph. At least mine seems to. When I was recovering from a crash, living in a neck/upper body brace, the only thing I could do was trust. I knew my life had value, because I was still alive. Understanding that life is fleeting, we get to ask ourselves, if the clothes we wear or the things we make for dinner really mean that much in the grand scheme of things.

Prayer:
Dear Heavenly Father, I value your faith in me. Stressing out should be my first response and I'm trying more and more to allow you to take control. Today, I will pause and breath, because I do trust you with everything. In your name. Amen.

Reflection:

Have you ever stopped to think about how valuable you are? Not because of the things you do or have, but simply because you're a child of God. Allow yourself the time to slow down, reflect, and journal on what you value most in life.

 *Trust*

Here's the scoop: Our plans might fall short, but God's got the master plan. Trust His course, and you'll be golden.

Proverbs 19:21 LOLV

Interpretation:
No matter what other people may think, no one knows our soul, our hearts, our desires like our Father God does. He knows what ignites our hearts and calms our souls. To be fair, he's still going to challenge you, but he's never going to trick us, or try to pull the wool over our eyes. It's a matter of us trusting him, his instructions, and the plan he has for us.

Prayer:
Dear Jesus, As I say yes to the master plan you have set for me please help me to stay strong and steadfast on the road of life, trusting that you know best. In your name. Amen.

Reflection:

Do you ever wonder what your next adventure might be? Do you find yourself trusting in the plans God has for you or questioning what's going to happen next? How might you be able to better trust that God is leading you?

 *Wisdom*

Sisters, choose wisdom as your walking companion, for a companion of fools will lead to harm.

Proverbs 13:20 LOLV

Interpretation:
Do you walk with fools? For real though, do you choose to walk with like-minded people, or people who have different priorities and beliefs than you? Do you choose to listen to the people just living day-to-day with no dreams, or are you walking with the ones that are just crazy enough to dream of changing the world? It's amazing, the harm that comes from living a life that is not our own, walking with companions that are no where near as fabulous as our Lord and savior.

Prayer:
Dear Father, Your companionship means the world to me. Following the fools of the world has only led to harm and I know walking with you is what's best for me. I reach out to you for the wisdom that I seek. In your name. Amen.

Reflection:

It's a scary world out there. Who are you walking with? Have you walked with fools? Are you trying to be someone else or are you content being who God created you to be? What obstacles in your past have harmed you? Moving forward, sister, let's walk together with the Lord, he really is the best companion a girl could ever want.

 *Power*

Sisters, God's power is on display. He's got a mighty hand, crafting the heavens and the earth. Talk about a divine artist!

Jeremiah 32:19 LOLV

Interpretation:
Jeremiah said it best about God's power, how does this apply to you though? Simple. Every time you are hurt, upset, or feeling pity, the story maker upstairs provides his power to you, to get past that pain and nudge you to be the person he created you to be. That's true power. Sis, some people will never see your true power, run from those folks and seek out the people who do.

Prayer:
Lord, my power comes from you. Period. Honestly, in the wrong hands, power can be pretty scary, but I trust you to use your almighty hands to keep me in the light when my flame may threaten to blow out. Please help to protect those I care about. In your name. Amen.

Reflection:

Deep down in all of us, we have access to God's power. He covers us in armor, ready for anything that may come out way. With all that protection behind you, how are you using your power? How are you making a difference? The sky's the limit when it comes to the things you can accomplish. Where might you be a year from now if you take the steps to fully embrace the power you have through God?

 *Faith*

Job let out a deep pained breath and explained to his friends, "You can't seriously be suggesting that I argue with God. He's profound and powerful. He can move mountains, shake the earth, and turn the sun off with a snap of his fingers. Do you see me? I'm mortal, I'm broken, and I'm basically dead. He could squash me right where I am without even breaking a sweat."

Job 9:2-20 LOLV

Interpretation:
Have you ever found yourself arguing with God? Doesn't work out too well does it. No matter what situation we find ourselves in, we get to remember that God is always in control. We get to have faith that he knows what he's doing, and no matter how much things might not make sense to us, God has a plan. And, when the time is right, he'll share that plan with us. Our job is to have faith, patience, and trust in God.

Prayer:
Dear God, Please understand that I'm trying to be faithful and not question the plans you have for me. There are times where I need you to remind me, that you have things under control. In your name. Amen.

Reflection:

When was the last time you experienced something in life that drove you to the edge? When you found yourself questioning what God was doing, or that he really was in control. How can you better remind yourself to stay faithful in God and his plan?

 *Focus*

Ladies, here's the scoop: Keeping your mind focused on the Lord brings perfect peace. Trust in Him forever, 'cause the Lord God? He's your everlasting rock, your solid foundation.

Isaiah 26:3-4 LOLV

Interpretation:
Think about the foundation of your house.It's what supports the entire building. It's what makes sure you aren't sleeping in mud, or sharing your kitchen with rodents. A strong foundation keeps your walls standing, your home warm, and pesky intruders out. Well, God does that for us. He's our foundation and when we focus on him, our foundation strengthens, better protecting us against anything or anyone that may seek to cause us harm.

Prayer:
Dear Heavenly Father, Please help me to stay focused on you, my relationship with you, and the ways you're always protecting me against the evils of the world. It's in you that I find everlasting peace. In your name. Amen.

Reflection:

Take a few moments and think back on the last week. What have you been focused on? Has it been things that have been going well? Or are you focused on where things aren't working out the way you'd like them to? How can you better refocus on your connection with God?

Armor

Sisters, stand tall! The Lord is your strength and shield, and your heart can trust in Him. Let joy be your anthem; He's got you covered.

Psalm 28:7 LOLV

Interpretation:
God talks a lot about putting on armor. Piece by piece he details how we can prepare for the day, especially those days when we're going to be dealing with difficult situations. What we forget though is that God takes care of us, he created us with armor already in place, all we need to do is trust and have faith that no matter what we face, God really does have our back.

Prayer:
Dear Heavenly Father, Thank you for creating me, ready for battle no matter how big or small. The strength you've provided me with in all things, gives me the backup I need to press on. In your name. Amen.

Reflection:

Metaphorically, do you put on armor when you're getting ready for the day? Some of us use makeup, a certain outfit, hairstyle, piece of jewelry, or our vehicle. What do you feel, when you put on your pieces of armor? How might you be able to better feel this confidence and strength with only the armor God has already given us?

 *Affection*

Dear ones, let your love be real. Detest evil, hold fast to good, and shower one another with sisterly affection. Let's outshine each other in showing honor, creating a beautiful tapestry of love.

Romans 12:9-10 LOLV

Interpretation:
So often in life we hear about people being love-bombed, or inundated with appreciation that isn't authentic or genuine. As children of God though, the love and affection we receive from him is always 100% the real deal. And, as his children, we get to spread that affection to the people in our own lives, and by doing so, honor God.

Prayer:
Dear Heavenly Father, Thank you for loving me and accepting me completely. I know that I'm not perfect, and definitely not always deserving of your affection, but you never leave me hanging. In your name. Amen.

Reflection:
How do you like to receive love from others? How do you most like to show your love for others? How can you better communicate your affection in a way that honors the love and affection God shows for you?

 *Peace*

Let Christ's peace be the boss of your hearts. It's what you were made for, part of this incredible sisterhood. And, oh, always be thankful.

Colossians 3:15 LOLV

Interpretation:
The peace we find through our faith in God is like nothing that can be experienced in any other way. He created us, perfectly, by design, to support, encourage, and flock to our sisters, our friends. For these things, we should always be grateful and appreciative.

Prayer:
Dear Lord, you've paved the way for me to live a life filled with anything and everything I could ever possibly desire. I bring to you my humanity, and ask that you continue to provide me with peace that only you offer. In your name. Amen.

Reflection:

When do you feel the most at peace? Is it when you're alone? Doing something you love? With friends, family, your fur-kids? A running theme throughout this devotional is peace, gratitude, and being perfectly made. God doesn't make mistakes ladies, everything about each and every one of us is by intentional design. That includes the phenomenal sisters he's surrounded us with.

 Thrive

Ladies, plant your roots by the waters, trust in the Lord. You'll flourish like a well-nourished tree, unshaken and thriving through every season.

Jeremiah 17:7-8 LOLV

Interpretation:
Early every season, farmers go out into their fields to start the process of prepping the soil and planting their crops. As a farmer myself, I'm no stranger to the process of nurturing my seedlings to ensure they root properly and have the opportunity to thrive. God does this with us, his children. He gives us the care and protection we need to take root, thrive, and grow stronger mentally, physically, emotionally, and spiritually.

Prayer:
Dear God, thank you for caring for and nurturing me. Without you I wouldn't be the strong, powerful woman I am today. In your name. Amen.

Reflection:

How do you nurture your own roots? What do you require to strengthen your physical, mental, emotional, and spiritual health? What can you do today to better thrive as the woman God has created you to be?

 Stress

Don't let stress be your heavy backpack. Instead, focus on the kind words you say to yourself. They can be like a burst of sunshine for the heart, lifting that weight right off.

Proverbs 12:25 LOLV

Interpretation:
No matter how heavy our load, as women, we often feel like we need to bear it alone. That asking for help, or splitting that load up into a few smaller trips, somehow makes us weak. Not true ladies. The key is understanding that while our load may be heavy, we may have a lot going on in our lives, we're never truly alone. Stress is a part of life, but we don't have to let it get us down, or cause us to be grumpy. Instead, take a deep breath, take a break, and speak kindly to yourself and others. God is always there beside us to help carry whatever load we may be struggling with.

Prayer:
Dear God, I don't know that I'll ever really understand why stress is a part of our world, but I trust that you have a reason for everything. Please help me while I go through my day, unpacking the heavy weight I carry on my back and better focusing on the kind words and sunshine within my life. In your name. Amen.

Reflection:

What stresses you out? What heavy weights burden you? Seriously, write them all down, all of it. Now, what causes you a burst of sunlight? When brings an instant smile to your face? How can you swap the two? Decreasing your stress and spending more time in the sun.

 *Whisper*

Don't let the world squeeze you into its mold. Instead, listen for the whispers from God, telling you all about his sweet plan – the good, the pleasing, and the perfect.

Romans 12:2 LOLV

Interpretation:
Too often we find ourselves trying desperately to fit into the mold or expectations of society, culture, the world when in reality, God has created us perfectly imperfect just as we are. In our own mold that was made with only us in mind. Next time you find yourself trying to be someone or something else, remember, God doesn't make mistakes, and listen for his whispers. They often come when we least expect them.

Prayer:
Dear God, Thank you for creating me just as I am, for never judging my shortcomings or the places where I feel like I may not be enough. I trust that you don't make mistakes and that I am one of your children. In your name. Amen.

Reflection:
Are you listening for God's whispers? They aren't always things we'll hear. Sometimes those whispers will come in the form of a conversation with a stranger, an experience you witness between friends, or something you see on TV. When was the last time you recognized a message that was sent to you from the man upstairs? How did the message come?

 **Masterpiece**

Girlfriend, here's the sweet truth: God works all things together for the good of those who love Him. Your story? It's part of His masterpiece.

Romans 8:28 LOLV

Interpretation:
Leonardo da Vinci created masterpieces that are still adored today. We ooh & ahh at one mans' creations as they hang in buildings around the world. God wants us to embrace our own stories, our own lives, for the epic masterpieces they are. Seriously ladies. God has our back. We are all a part of his divine plan. He's proud of who you are. You have nothing to worry about when it comes to turning out how God expects you to. Your story, it's part of an even bigger plan, one that was written before you were born.

Prayer:
Dear Heavenly Father, Allow me to see all of the work you've done with and for me. Please help me to understand all of the attention you've paid to the creation of me and my life, as your masterpiece. I am so thankful for your love and even when I make choices or mistakes that challenge your plan, please know that I will always come back to you. In your name. Amen.

Reflection:

So, what's your story? Take a few moments to reflect on your unique story, your choices, your lived experiences thus far. How have these contributed to your life, your masterpiece thus far?

www.ingramcontent.com/pod-product-compliance
Lightning Source LLC
Chambersburg PA
CBHW051259120626
46547CB00015B/2014